W9-CKL-990

Booker T. Washington

Civil Rights Leader and Education Advocate

Avery Elizabeth Hurt

Cavendish
Square

New York

Published in 2020 by Cavendish Square Publishing, LLC
243 5th Avenue, Suite 136, New York, NY 10016

Library of Congress Cataloging-in-Publication Data

Names: Hurt, Avery Elizabeth, author.
Title: Booker T. Washington : civil rights leader and education advocate / Avery Elizabeth Hurt.
Description: First edition. | New York : Cavendish Square, [2020] |
Series: African American trailblazers | Includes bibliographical references and index.
Identifiers: LCCN 2018047437 (print) | LCCN 2018051209 (ebook) | ISBN 9781502645593 (ebook) |
ISBN 9781502645586 (library bound) | ISBN 9781502645579 (pbk.)
Subjects: LCSH: Washington, Booker T., 1856-1915--Juvenile literature. |
African Americans--Biography--Juvenile literature. | Educators--United States--
Biography--Juvenile literature. | Tuskegee Institute--Juvenile literature.
Classification: LCC E185.97.W4 (ebook) | LCC E185.97.W4 H87 2020 (print) | DDC 370.92 [B] --dc23
LC record available at https://lccn.loc.gov/2018047437

Editorial Director: David McNamara
Editor: Kristen Susienka
Copy Editor: Alex Tessman
Associate Art Director: Alan Sliwinski
Designer: Joe Parenteau
Production Coordinator: Karol Szymczuk
Photo Research: J8 Media

Printed in the United States of America

CONTENTS

INTRODUCTION

From Cabin to Campus

Today we know him as Booker T. Washington, but when he was a child, he was known only as Booker. He was born a slave in 1856, slightly before the start of the Civil War. Only after he and his people were freed a little more than a decade later would he choose for himself a last name and discover that his mother had given him a middle name (Taliaferro) when he was born.

Longing for Education

Young Booker wasn't bothered much by the fact that he had no last name, but he was much troubled by not being allowed to learn. Slaves were not allowed to attend

Booker T. Washington was a striking man with a distinguished character. For much of his adulthood he advocated for education for all African Americans.

school or even learn to read, and Washington longed for education.

When the war was over and the slaves were set free, Washington finally had a chance at education, though it wasn't easy. He made great sacrifices in order to learn. He stayed up late at night after work studying, and he walked long distances to meet with teachers. Eventually, he graduated from college and immediately began teaching others. He would found one of the nation's most successful historically black colleges, what is now Tuskegee University. He would become one of the nation's most beloved and respected educators. In his later years, he was the acknowledged leader of the African American community.

Establishing Purpose

Washington's purpose in life was to help African Americans become successful in the post-slavery world. The years just after emancipation were hard, and it would be many more before the majority of whites accepted

Booker T. Washington (*standing*) addresses students and administrators at Tuskegee University.

blacks as equal citizens. After 1865, many whites, especially in the South where most blacks lived, were actively hostile to their recently freed fellow Americans. Laws to protect blacks and give them political rights were ignored, and other laws were passed to restrict their rights and freedoms.

Guiding his people through these difficult years was a challenge for Washington. He believed that economic independence and entrepreneurship were essential if African Americans were to survive. Constitutional amendments made blacks voting citizens and guaranteed them the protection of the law. Still, white people were in charge, and during Washington's lifetime there was little blacks could do to protect their rights and protect themselves from violence by hostile whites. Washington resisted activities that further antagonized whites and advised his fellow blacks to work hard to get along with whites and not demand political and social equality.

He believed that blacks should concentrate first on education and entrepreneurship. When they owned land and businesses and had proved themselves both capable and necessary to the white economy, only then would they be ready for political action and involvement. His tremendous success at Tuskegee proved the value of his approach, and by far most African Americans agreed with his methods. However, some thought that he was too accepting of injustice and too slow to demand change. In his later years, he was reviled by some younger black leaders, such as W. E. B. Du Bois. He was accused of being a sell-out and of holding back his race. Nevertheless, his work in education and his tireless efforts to give African Americans a sense of dignity and self-worth helped create a black middle class and make possible the generation that launched and led the civil rights movement of the 1950s and 1960s, decades after Washington's death.

Today many people still wonder if Washington did more good than harm. Might civil rights for blacks have come earlier if he had been less accommodating of white power? Or did his slow and measured approach prepare and protect his people until the time was right for the movement? Historians do not agree, but there is no denying Booker T. Washington helped many African Americans out of poverty and that he is an inspiration to people, both black and white, even today.

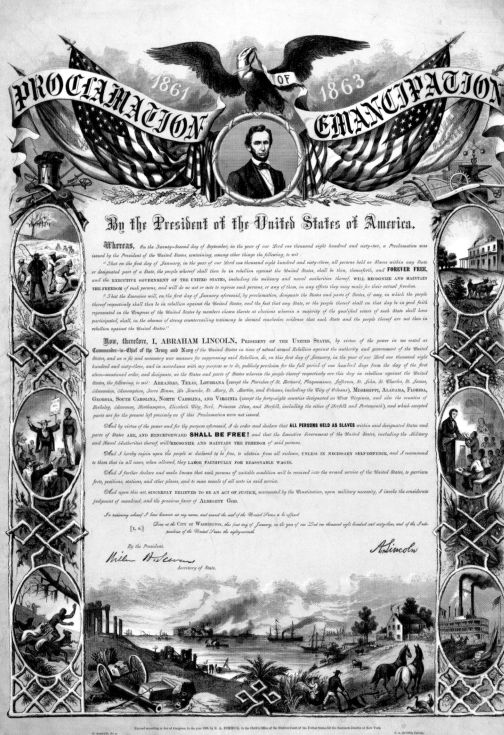

CHAPTER ONE

*Freedom and
Its Challenges*

I n 1865, when Booker T. Washington was a boy of nine years old, the Civil War ended, and for the first time in his life, he was no longer a slave. Though they were released from bondage, freedmen (as former slaves were called) faced a completely new set of problems. They had no land, no way to support themselves, and were living in a society filled with people who weren't particularly happy to see them free. It was this situation that Washington worked within, dealt with, and tried to overcome for the rest of his life.

The Emancipation Proclamation was signed by President Abraham Lincoln on January 1, 1863.

Free at Last

In December 1865, the Thirteenth Amendment was added to the United States Constitution, abolishing slavery throughout the nation. In 1868, the Fourteenth Amendment guaranteed equal protection of the law to all citizens born or naturalized in the United States, including former slaves. The Fifteenth Amendment, ratified in 1870, gave black men the right to vote. (Women of any color were not guaranteed the right to vote until 1920, when the Nineteenth Amendment was ratified.)

These amendments, often called the Reconstruction amendments, provided a legal framework for protecting the rights of blacks and former slaves. Slaves were now free, full citizens entitled to the same protections of the law that any other citizen got. They could take part in the affairs of their nation by voting or holding public office. Or at least that was the intent of these amendments. In reality, however, things were quite different for the almost four million people who were freed by the ending of the Civil War.

Malice Toward None

After the Civil War, the challenge for the nation was how to reintegrate the states that had seceded from the Union to form the Confederacy. Freed slaves were not the only people whose citizenship needed to be decided. Would citizens of the former Confederacy be immediately restored to full citizenship in the United States? Would rebel states be treated as states no different from the ones that did not secede? Or would the region be an occupied territory in which the federal government would oversee a gradual re-assimilation and make sure that the laws of the nation were respected in the South as well as in the North?

Abraham Lincoln, who was the US president throughout the war and at its end, favored a quick reunion. The Southern states were to be forgiven for their treachery and accepted back as full and equal members of the nation. Less than a year after Abraham Lincoln signed the Emancipation Proclamation, declaring the freedom of slaves, he introduced a plan for reintegrating the rebel states into the nation. According to Lincoln's Amnesty Proclamation (issued in December 1863, a little over a year before the end of the war), any state would be readmitted and allowed to form state governments if 10 percent of its voters would swear allegiance to the United States *and* if the state would abolish slavery. (This proposal was made before the Thirteenth Amendment was passed.)

Not everyone thought this was a good idea. A horrific war had just been fought and almost seven hundred thousand soldiers (and some historians estimate as many as fifty thousand civilians) had died because of the policies and actions of the rebel states. Some people believed that because the Southern states had committed treason and voluntarily left the nation, they should, now that the Union had won the war, be treated like a conquered nation. Such lenient terms as Lincoln proposed might end up putting power right back into the hands of the Southern aristocracy that caused the war in the first place. Indeed, when white Southerners were allowed to vote for representatives to Congress, many of the men they chose were former Confederate leaders and generals.

Lincoln's position was both lawyerly and political. The lawyer in him did not consider that the Southern states had ever left the nation, because they weren't legally able to do so. He had waged a war at least in part to prove this point. The politician in him believed that reuniting the nation as rapidly and as smoothly as possible was the most essential point.

THE EMANCIPATION PROCLAMATION

By 1863, the United States was slogging into its third year of the bloody Civil War. There had been a great deal of debate up to this point about whether freeing slaves in the Confederate states was a necessary or even prudent goal of the war. However, when President Abraham Lincoln issued the Emancipation Proclamation on January 1, 1863, it became crystal clear what the position of the United States was regarding slavery. The document stated that "all persons held as slaves ... shall be ... forever free."[1]

This did not exactly free the slaves, however. It applied only to the states that had rebelled against the United States. The border states that were slave states but had not seceded were exempt. It also excused those states or parts of Confederate states that were under Union control. Perhaps most important, it hinged on one very important factor: the United States winning the war. The Confederate states, which the proclamation targeted, were not about to free their slaves, and the war was not over yet.

Despite these details, the Emancipation Proclamation did clearly state that the intention of the United States was to abolish slavery. It also provided for the acceptance of black men in the United States Army and Navy (which would be a big factor in the eventual Union victory). Perhaps most important, it stated once and for all that the war was not just about preserving the Union.

When the United States won, the reunited nation was a truly free one. In January 1865, a few months before the end of the war, Congress passed the Thirteenth Amendment to the US Constitution, formally outlawing slavery. It was ratified by the states on December 6, 1865.

This portrait of Abraham Lincoln was taken by Matthew Brady. It is an iconic image of a man who is much remembered in US history today.

In 1862, before issuing the Emancipation Proclamation, which confirmed that the Civil War was being fought to end slavery, Lincoln gave his annual address to Congress. In it, he stressed the importance of keeping the Union together, no matter what was done about the slaves. After a lengthy list of the various proposals about what to do about freed slaves, Lincoln said, "Because of these diversities we waste much strength in struggles among ourselves. By mutual concession we should harmonize and act together."[2] Once the war was won, Lincoln had no desire to punish those who had taken part in the insurrection. In his second inaugural address, given in March 1865, just as the war was ending, Lincoln urged his fellow Americans to "bind up the nation's wounds" with "malice toward none, with charity for all."[3]

Resisting Reconstruction

We will never know how Lincoln would have handled Reconstruction, the period of federal involvement in the former Confederate states that lasted from the end of the war until 1877. He did not live to deal with the problem. Andrew Johnson became president when Lincoln was assassinated just a few days after the formal end of the war.

Johnson, a Southerner himself, agreed that former members of the Confederacy should be forgiven. He granted blanket pardons to all Southern whites, except for Confederate political and military leaders. Eventually, many of these would be granted individual pardons. He put military governors in charge of the Southern states until they could reestablish their own governments.

Many of the federal initiatives during this Reconstruction period were an attempt to help establish freed slaves in society

Andrew Johnson, circa 1865. He became president upon the assassination of Lincoln in April 1865, and he had to lead the nation through the difficult postwar period.

and protect them from former slave owners. Not long before the end of the war, Congress established what it called the Freedmen's Bureau. This was intended to help slaves as they adjusted to freedom. The Freedmen's Bureau provided food and medical care and operated schools for former slaves. It also established special courts to settle disputes between black workers and white employers. White Southerners resented these federal interventions in their society.

Johnson himself was not terribly keen on extending citizenship rights to former slaves. He was eager to get state governments up and running and free of federal control as soon as possible. His plan for establishing state governments did not allow blacks to vote for delegates to the state conventions that would create new state constitutions, nor were blacks allowed to participate in any way in the process. Basically, according to Johnson's view of Reconstruction, the former Confederate states were free to run their states however they liked as long as they abolished slavery and remained loyal to the nation. Blacks would play no part in governing.

Not surprisingly, as soon as the Southern states had established their own governments, they immediately began to pass laws that severely limited the rights of blacks and ensured white supremacy. These were called black codes. Black codes actually gave some rights to blacks. Former slaves could buy and sell property, enter into contracts, and be paid for work. Their marriages were recognized as legal and their children legitimate. (However, marriages between a black person and a white person were not legal in most states. The Supreme Court did not rule that interracial marriages were legal until 1967. Alabama did not take its law against such marriages off the books until 2000.) Other laws seemed to be attempts to establish a system not much different from slavery. At the very least, they reinforced white supremacy and limited economic opportunity for blacks.

In some states, black employees had to sign a contract in which they were "servants" who worked for "masters." If they quit before the end of their contract, they could be arrested and returned to the "master" and forced to finish out the term of the contract. White employers could whip their adult black servants if they had the approval of a judge (who was, of course, also white). They needed no approval to whip servants who were younger than eighteen years old. It was better than slavery, but not enough better.

Jim Crow Comes to Town

After the Fifteenth Amendment gave black men the right to vote, a Congress was elected that was much less obliging to the Southern states. Congress instituted its own Reconstruction plan. This one forced Southern states to allow black men to vote, and some blacks were even elected to public office in the South. Many of the more outrageous provisions of the black codes were repealed. However, this phase of Reconstruction did not last long. Racist attitudes began to grow throughout the nation (not just in the South), and the rest of the country lost the will to help freed slaves. Black codes gave way to a new and much more widespread system of laws and customs designed to enforce white supremacy. It was called Jim Crow.

Over time, Jim Crow laws led to the separation of blacks and whites in many aspects of life. Black people were required to go to separate schools and use separate bathrooms and water fountains from whites. Blacks couldn't stay in white hotels or eat at white restaurants. They had to use separate libraries and medical clinics. They even had to be buried in a separate part

This café in Durham, North Carolina, in 1940 had separate entrances and seating for blacks and whites. This arrangement was typical of the Jim Crow era.

of cemeteries. Even in traffic, white drivers had the right of way over black drivers. Once vehicles were more popular on the roads, if a black person rode in the car of a white person, the black person had to ride in the back seat. If they were in a truck, the black person had to ride in the bed of the truck. Jim Crow was not just law, but customs. Blacks were expected to treat whites with respect; the favor was not, of course, returned. Blacks were expected to use courtesy titles, such as "mister" or "miss" and "sir" or "ma'am," when addressing whites, whereas whites always called blacks by their first names. Often a grown black man would simply be called "boy."

Violating Jim Crow could be very dangerous for blacks. Something as simple as using a white restroom could result in a beating—or worse—for a black person. Whites were particularly jumpy about anything that looked like an attempt at a relationship between a black man and a white woman. Many black men were beaten or killed simply for the crime of smiling at or speaking to a white woman.

Trying to vote was an especially risky move for Southern blacks during the years of Jim Crow. Though voting was a constitutionally guaranteed right, exercising that right could cost a black person his or her life.

The police, the juries, and the judges were all white. If a white person harmed or killed a black person, there would be no justice. And whites did kill blacks very often, and often very brutally. Lynchings, a kind of mob murder, usually by hanging, were very common in the decades after the Civil War. According to the NAACP (National Association for the Advancement of Colored People) between 1882 and 1968, over three thousand black men and women were lynched. It was a form of terrorism designed to intimidate blacks and make sure they were too frightened to demand their rights.

The Nation's Only Coup

Even when blacks did run for office, win elections, and gain some control of their cities and towns, they were not safe. In 1894, a coalition of populists and Republicans, called Fusionists, won the majority in the North Carolina General Assembly. Two years later, in 1896, the state elected a Republican governor. The Fusionists passed many laws to protect blacks and middle-class whites. In Wilmington, then the largest city in the state, blacks served on the city council and in the police department. It was not a fruitful environment for Jim Crow.

In the statewide election of 1898, the Democrats were determined to regain control of the state government and reverse this progress. They ran on a white supremacist platform, organized white supremacist rallies and parades, and instigated a program to intimidate black voters. Alfred Waddell, one of the most vocal white nationalist leaders, urged white voters to go to the polls, and if while there they saw a black person trying to vote, they should tell him to leave. If he didn't leave, Waddell said to "shoot him down in his tracks."[4] The intimidation worked, and the Democrats regained control of the state. Two days after the election, Waddell led a group of whites in the overthrow of the city government of Wilmington. They forced the elected officials to resign—at gunpoint—and named Waddell the mayor. Waddell's mob burned black businesses and banished wealthy and successful blacks from the city. It is not known exactly how many blacks were killed that day, but some estimates reach into the hundreds. It was a chilling warning to blacks who aimed for professional and business success and middle-class lives.

The new government of North Carolina and of Wilmington proceeded to pass laws to prevent blacks from voting and to institute all the evils of Jim Crow.

Going Backward

Racial hatred was at the bottom of a lot of this violence and discrimination. However, that hatred was fostered in the ways that hatred usually is—by insecurity and fear of change. The 1890s were a time of increased industrialization, urbanization, and economic instability throughout the country. Jobs were scarce and working-class whites did not want to have to compete with blacks for work. Southern farmers feared competition from newly freed slaves who were trying to start their own small farms. In the mid-1890s, gangs of white terrorists burned black farmers' homes and crops, sometimes even killing them.

In order to justify this hatred, whites convinced themselves that blacks were little more than animals. It was commonly believed that black people were inferior to whites intellectually and morally. In 1892, Virginia lawyer and author Thomas Nelson Page wrote, "The negro has not progressed, not because he was a slave, but because he does not possess the faculties to raise himself above slavery."[5] Many white people, both in the North and the South, believed this to be true.

The existence of educated and successful blacks, like those in Wilmington's government and business community, would seem to prove this for the nonsense it was. Yet that did nothing to change the views of white supremacists. Even, or perhaps especially, well-educated blacks were perceived to be a threat. Perhaps they were more of a threat to whites' sense of superiority than to their economic standing. Whatever the reason, in 1890, John Tyler Morgan, US senator from Alabama, tried to persuade the US government to launch a project to remove educated blacks from the South. They were, he said, "constantly armed with inveterate suspicions toward the white race."[6] It's not hard to imagine why they might have been suspicious.

This was the dismal situation Booker T. Washington found himself in as he began the task of leading his fellow African Americans. He was more than willing to work with whites, respect them, and even compromise if that's what it took to improve his life and that of his fellow African Americans. His approach seemed like timidity to some, like heroism to others. It began in a wretched slave cabin and ended in the presidential mansion of a well-respected university, and along the way changed many lives and influenced a nation.

CHAPTER TWO

The Great Educator

B ooker T. Washington was born in an unheated cabin that had no windows. He died in the president's mansion of a prestigious university. The road between the two was long and rewarding.

A Glimpse of Paradise

Washington was nine years old before he had more than one name. Until then, everyone just called him Booker. He was born a slave on a plantation in Franklin County, Virginia. He never knew who his father was, but he believed him to be a white man from a nearby plantation. Washington spent his first nine years living in a slave cabin with his

This slave cabin would be much like the one where Washington was born and spent his childhood.

mother, his brother, John, and sister, Amanda. His mother, Jane, was the cook for the plantation, and their cabin also served as the plantation's kitchen. She cooked in the small room over an open fire. There was no door and no windows, only openings in the walls. However, there was a hole in a back corner wall for cats to get in and out. When Washington was a boy, he wondered why there needed to be a hole for the cats when they could simply walk through the places where the doors and windows should have been. The lack of windows kept the place miserably cold in winter. The cook-fire kept it stiflingly hot in summer. In his autobiography, *Up from Slavery*, Washington recalls that he didn't sleep in a bed until after emancipation. Instead he and his siblings slept on a pallet of rags on the dirt floor of the cabin.

Washington was once asked what sorts of games and sports he enjoyed as a child. Until he was asked that question it had never occurred to him there was never a time in his life in which he just played. Instead he worked. He fetched water and ran errands. He carried corn to the mill to be ground into cornmeal. He recalls in his autobiography that bags of corn would be tossed across the back of a horse and he would be set on top. Inevitably the bags would slip off the horse—taking little Booker with them. He was far too small to lift the heavy bags back onto the horse. He would have to wait, sometimes for hours, for someone to come along and help him get himself and the corn back on the horse. Of course, because of this delay, he would be late for his errand and get a scolding, or worse.

Washington did not realize that he was missing out on play. However, he did realize that he was missing out on education. Sometimes he would have to carry the schoolbooks for one of the white children who lived on the plantation. He recalled getting a glimpse of the other children at school: "The picture of several dozen boys and girls in a schoolroom engaged in study made a deep impression upon me, and I had the feeling that to get into a schoolhouse and study in this way would be about the same as getting into paradise."[1]

Even though slaves were not allowed to learn to read and had little to no access to newspapers even if they could, they still managed to stay well-informed of the great events going on in the nation around them. They heard a lot of gossip—what Washington called "the grape vine." In the case of Washington's community, the slave who was sent to town to pick up the mail would linger at the post office and listen to the white men talking about the latest news of the war. Then he would rush home and spread the word among his fellow slaves. Washington said that often the slaves would hear the results of the latest battles before the people at the plantation house did. He recalled awakening one night to find his mother "kneeling over her children and fervently praying that Lincoln and his armies might be successful, and that one day she and her children might be free."[2]

Her prayers were answered. In 1865, the Confederate States of America surrendered to the United States, and all the slaves were freed. For the first time in his life, Booker T. Washington could get an education.

School at Last

Freedom for Washington did not mean a life of ease. In fact, it meant more labor, and it was even more backbreaking. However, life in Malden, West Virginia, where he lived after the war, offered the fulfillment of one of Washington's greatest dreams. It was there that he learned to read.

Washington's mother was married to a slave who belonged to another plantation. At the end of the war, he was living in Malden. Jane took her children and joined her husband. By the

This camp, provided by the Union army, gave shelter to newly freed slaves who had been granted their freedom but had no money and no homes.

time his family arrived, Washington's stepfather had gotten a job at a local salt mine. He put Washington and his brother John to work there too. It was very hard work. Washington often started his workday at four in the morning. He did not lose his desire for education, however. He persuaded his mother to get him a book, and she managed, somehow, to find for him an old school spelling book. Because there were no teachers available and neither of his parents could read, Washington used the book to teach himself to read. Soon, the little community of freed slaves decided to start a school. An educated black man from Ohio came to teach the students.

Keeping up with his studies was no problem for Washington. However, there was a problem about his name. Before starting school, it had never occurred to him that he needed any more name than simply Booker. However, when the roll was called in school, the other children had two names, a first and a last—some of them even had three names, which Washington described as an "extravagance."[3] When the teacher asked for his name, he came up with something on the spot. "Booker Washington" he said. Later, when he told his mother about this, she told him that when he was born she had named him Booker Taliaferro (pronounced "Toliver"), but somewhere along the way his second name had been lost. So he added Taliaferro and was henceforth known as Booker Taliaferro Washington. "I think there are not many men in our country who have had the privilege of naming themselves in the way that I have," he wrote.[4]

The Promised Land

Sadly, Washington was not able to stay in school for long. He had to work during the day, in a coal mine by this time, and could not get away for classes. He was determined, however, and sought out teachers who could teach him in the evenings. Sometimes he had to walk several miles to find a teacher. One day, while working in the coal mine, he heard some people talking about a school that was much better than the little community school he had briefly attended. Not only was this school a much better one, but talented students were allowed to earn their tuition by working for the school. This would also give students a chance to learn a trade. It was the Hampton Normal and Agricultural Institute (now Hampton University). Washington had no idea where it was or how to get there, but he was determined that he would.

Meanwhile, he got a job working in the household of the Ruffner family, who owned the local salt and coal mines. Mrs. Viola Ruffner was very strict, and most of the boys who worked for her did not stay long. She demanded that everything be kept perfectly clean and orderly. Washington was very comfortable with that and carried these habits with him for the rest of his life. Later, when he was a teacher himself, he stressed above almost anything else the virtue of being clean and tidy.

He lived with the Ruffners for about a year and half. During this time, Washington and Mrs. Ruffner became good friends. She made sure he had a chance to attend classes and read. Later he recalled, "Mrs. Ruffner always encouraged and sympathized with me in all my efforts to get an education. It was while living with her that I began to get together my first library. I secured a dry-goods box, knocked out one side of it, put some shelves in it, and began putting into it every kind of book that I could get my hands upon, and called it my 'library.'"[5] Washington was still determined to study at Hampton. In 1872, when he was just sixteen years old, he set out for Hampton with a cheap suitcase, a few articles of

The campus of Hampton University as it appears today. Historically a black university, it was founded in 1868 in Hampton, Virginia.

clothing, and meager savings supplemented by donations of dimes and nickels given to him by older freed blacks who supported his ambitions.

It turned out the school was in Virginia, about 500 miles (805 kilometers) away. He began his trip on a stagecoach. When the coach stopped for the night at a hotel, Washington's

fellow passengers, who were all white, secured rooms for the night. When Washington approached the sign-in desk, however, he was turned away. The hotel did not allow blacks to stay there. In one way, it was just as well. He couldn't afford the cost of the room, anyway. He couldn't afford the stagecoach either. For the rest of the trip, he walked, occasionally begging rides on the back of a wagon.

When he reached Richmond, some 82 miles (132 km) into his journey, he was exhausted and hungry. He had spent the tiny amount of money he had on food. He spotted a ship unloading iron and asked the captain if he could work enough to earn money for his breakfast. The captain agreed and was so pleased with Washington's work that he let the industrious young man work for several more days. Washington made enough to buy some food and save a little bit for food for the rest of the journey. He made it to Hampton with fifty cents in his pocket.

When he saw the college's buildings, he recalled, "I felt that a new kind of existence had now begun—that life would now have a new meaning. I felt that I had reached the promised land, and I resolved to let no obstacle prevent me from putting forth the highest effort to fit myself to accomplish the most good in the world."[6]

Of course, arriving didn't mean being admitted. After his long journey, Washington didn't look or smell very promising. Mary F. Mackie, the woman in charge of admitting students, didn't turn him away, but she didn't admit him either. When after several hours Washington was still hanging around, she finally told him to go sweep the recitation room. His time with Mrs. Ruffner was about to pay off. As he recalled in his autobiography:

> It occurred to me at once that here was my chance. Never did I receive an order with more delight. I knew that I could sweep, for Mrs. Ruffner had thoroughly taught me how to do that when I lived with her. I swept the recitation-room three times. Then I got a dusting-cloth and dusted it four times. All the woodwork around the walls, every bench, table, and desk, I went over four times with my dusting-cloth … I had the feeling that in a large measure my future depended upon the impression I made upon the teacher in the cleaning of that room.[7]

It worked. Not only was he admitted to the college, he was given a position as a janitor at the school so that he was able to earn his keep. It was the perfect job for Mrs. Ruffner's former employee.

Umbrellas Indoors

Washington did well at Hampton. He graduated in 1875 with honors and returned to Malden to teach at the colored school there. He was determined to use his education to help other freedmen and women get a better life. He used his earnings, in part, to help his brothers attend Hampton as well. (His family had adopted another little boy not long after they moved to Malden.) John, his older brother, had helped in whatever small way he could with Booker's expenses while he was in school.

After teaching in Malden for two years, Washington went to Washington, DC, to continue his education. He studied at the Wayland Seminary for eighteen months. After that, he returned to Hampton, this time as a teacher. He worked as head of Hampton's Native American boys school. In this position he was able to find time to continue his studies. Soon, however, Washington was offered another opportunity. The head of Hampton, Samuel Armstrong, was asked to recommend a white teacher for the job of principal and administrator of a new teacher training school in Tuskegee, Alabama. Armstrong recommended Washington, who he thought better for the job than any of the white teachers at Hampton.

The people in Alabama responded quickly. Washington would suit them. He was asked to come to Tuskegee as soon as possible.

When Washington arrived in Tuskegee in early summer of 1881, he found a town of around two thousand people, about half of whom were black. What he did not find, however, was a school. There were plenty of students, ready and eager to learn, but no building or facilities for teaching them. There was also no money, except for a small amount the Alabama legislature had designated to pay teachers.

The man who had made his way from Malden to Hampton with almost no money and no transportation, and had worked his way through college when he got there, was not disheartened by this problem. He began living and teaching in a dilapidated

Here, a group of male students at Tuskegee University use bricks they have made themselves to build the campus's classrooms and other buildings.

building that housed the local black church, and the equally ramshackle building next door. The buildings were so leaky that when it rained, his landlady had to hold an umbrella over his head while he ate breakfast.

Because the only money appropriated for the school had to be used to pay teachers, Washington borrowed $250 from Armstrong. He used this as a down payment on a worn-out piece of land on the outskirts of Tuskegee. It was an abandoned plantation, about 100 acres (40.5 hectares), with a burned-out plantation house and a few rundown cabins and outbuildings. Washington organized the students to build their own school on this property. They built a kiln, made bricks, and built buildings from them. In only two years, they had a classroom building, a dining hall, a girls' dormitory, and a chapel. They also made bricks to sell to earn money for other necessities of the college.

After a wobbly start, the school thrived under Washington's leadership. By 1888 it was officially called the Tuskegee Normal and Industrial Institute and had more than four hundred students enrolled. By that time, Washington had expanded the campus to 540 acres (218.5 ha). Because the students studied industrial and agricultural subjects as well as reading, writing, and mathematics, they were able to meet most of their own needs. Students grew and cooked their own food and made and repaired their own clothes. They were taught nutrition, food preservation, and basic health and hygiene. Students at Tuskegee learned virtually all the trades, from carpentry and farming to printing and masonry. It was Washington's intention to give his students the skills they needed to succeed economically. He believed that in order for a race that had been oppressed for hundreds of years to prosper, it would need to be self-sufficient. He realized, however, that people who had only recently been released from generations of bondage had many obstacles to overcome. He did not mislead his students into thinking it would be easy. He did, however, offer great support and encouragement. Washington often spoke to the students at chapel on Sunday evenings. In one of those talks, he said:

> Every person who has grown to any degree of usefulness, every person who has grown to distinction, almost without exception has been a person who has risen by overcoming obstacles, by removing difficulties, by resolving that when he met discouragements he would not give up … Make up your minds that your future is just as bright as that of anybody else. Do this, and you will find that you have it in your own power to make your future bright or gloomy, just as you desire.[8]

Passing the Hat

Not everything a college needs can be made from brick or grown in the fields. Operating such a large school required funds. Washington proved to be a master fundraiser. First, he had to repay the loan he took out for the property. He and Olivia Davidson, the assistant principal of the school (and his future wife), organized festivals. They canvassed the local community for donations of food items—cakes, pies, chickens—that they then sold to raise money. Tuskegee's population, both white and black, were generous. Those who had little gave what they could. Some gave a few coins, some shared eggs, or even a quilt. However, the local community was far too poor to provide the kind of support a school like this needed.

Abolitionists in the Northeast donated funds, but soon Washington and his school attracted wealthier support.

Washington quickly developed a national reputation as a first-rate and innovative educator. He spoke at national education conferences and held programs and meetings at the Tuskegee campus. The work he was doing there, and his ability to communicate his ideas and methods, attracted the attention of many wealthy white philanthropists who supported his work. Industrialist Andrew Carnegie and Julius Rosenwald, one of the founders of the retail giant Sears, Roebuck and Company, were among Tuskegee's most generous supporters. Philanthropic foundations, such as the Peabody Education Fund and the John F. Slater Fund, also contributed generously to the cause of African American education.

Neither Preacher nor Politician

Washington liked to point out that unlike many black leaders, he was neither a politician nor a preacher, but a businessman. And indeed it was his skills at organizing and running a large operation that made Tuskegee Institute successful and attracted the attention of wealthy businessmen. In 1900, Washington founded the National Negro Business League. Washington believed that the lives of African Americans could be improved by bettering their economic conditions, and that blacks could and should do this for themselves. The organization promoted and supported black-owned businesses in and out of the South. Washington's idea was that one way for blacks to deal with the Jim Crow South was to have their own strong and successful businesses and communities.

Washington's business and organizational success led to political influence as well. Presidents of other colleges and presidents of the United States came to Booker T. Washington for advice on how to help poor Southerners, black and white.

He received honorary degrees from Dartmouth and Harvard Universities. Presidents William McKinley and Theodore Roosevelt visited Tuskegee, and Washington dined at the White House with Roosevelt. Washington twice visited Europe and met with many dignitaries there, including Queen Victoria.

Frederick Douglass, the escaped slave who became a leader in the abolitionist movement and then in the fight for civil rights for blacks, had been for many years the leader of the African American community. As Douglass grew older (he died in 1895), Washington was considered by many to be the natural heir to this leadership position. That same year, Washington gave a speech that for many African Americans proved that he was their natural leader. However, the speech also gave ammunition to many of his critics and rivals, including African American leader W. E. B. Du Bois. In this speech, Washington said that blacks and whites should remain separate, and indicated that blacks were not yet ready for political equality.

Du Bois saw the speech as accepting the black race as inferior. Washington, meanwhile, was undoubtedly willing to accept, at least temporarily, a separate but equal status for African Americans. This was a complicated disagreement in which both men played a role in shaping the future of the African American community.

Despite these criticisms and conflicts, Washington's work and his influence were huge. In addition to his popular autobiography *Up from Slavery*, he wrote many other books, speeches, and articles. He was respected and even beloved by Americans, both black and white. And he never lost sight of his life's work.

By the twenty-fifth anniversary of the Tuskegee Institute, the campus included 2,000 acres (809 ha) and eighty-three buildings. The college had an endowment of over $1 million

SECOND IN COMMAND

Olivia Davidson was Washington's beloved second wife. Some historians believe that Washington was closer to her and fonder of her than of his other two wives. However, theirs was more than just a romantic relationship. She was effectively Washington's second-in-command at Tuskegee during her years there. She must be given at least some of the credit for the great success of the school.

Davidson was born in Virginia. Her father was an ex-slave and her mother was freeborn. Her family moved to Ohio when she was still a young child. She attended the Enterprise Academy in Albany, Ohio. This was a pioneering school run by abolitionists and black educators. Not only was her education there exceptional, she had the advantage of meeting and talking with many black intellectuals and leaders. Albany was a stop on the Underground Railroad, and many black activists lived in the area.

She began teaching when she was still young, and soon after the end of the Civil War she moved to Mississippi to teach former slaves. In 1878, she enrolled in Hampton Normal and Agricultural Institute. It was there she met her future husband, when he came back there to teach after his graduation in 1875. They did not marry, however, until some years later.

Davidson was a great advocate for the education of women. In 1886, she spoke to the Alabama State Teacher Association on the topic "How Shall We Make the Women of Our Race Stronger?" She firmly believed that African American women were the hope of the race. Tuskegee under her and Washington's leadership was a pioneer venture in the education of women, graduating them alongside the men.

At Tuskegee, in addition to teaching, Davidson served as the head of the women's division, developed curriculum, and was very involved in fundraising. Her death in 1889 from tuberculosis was a blow not only to Washington but to the entire Tuskegee community.

Olivia Davidson Washington helped Washington build and develop the school at Tuskegee. She was particularly active in the education and empowerment of black women.

Here is Washington's grave and marker on the campus of Tuskegee University.

and enrolled just over 1,500 students. The face of education for blacks had been changed forever. Many of the people who would later become leaders in the civil rights movement of the 1950s and 1960s owe much of their education to Booker T. Washington, whether or not they attended Tuskegee.

Home at Last

In 1882, not long after moving to Tuskegee, Washington married Fannie Norton Smith, a woman he had fallen in love with back home in Malden. They had one daughter, Portia

Washington. Sadly, Smith died two years later while Portia was still an infant. In 1885, Washington married again, this time Olivia Davidson, Tuskegee's assistant principal who had also studied at Hampton. Washington and Davidson had two children, Booker Taliaferro Washington Jr. and Ernest Davidson Washington. Olivia Davidson Washington died in 1889. In 1893, Washington married, for the third and last time. His new wife was Margaret James Murray. She directed programs for female students at the institute.

After many years of working hard at home and traveling the nation on behalf of the Tuskegee Institute and his fellow African Americans, Washington's health began to deteriorate. On November 5, 1915, he was hospitalized while on a business trip to New York. He was suffering from exhaustion and heart disease. Knowing that he was not likely to survive, he asked to go home. His wife, Margaret, and his physician accompanied him back to Tuskegee, where he died at home on November 14. Eight thousand people attended his funeral, and he was buried on campus in a tomb built by Tukegee students.

CHAPTER THREE

Presidents and Robber Barons

In order to build and operate the Tuskegee Institute and pursue his goals of improving the lives of African Americans through economic opportunities, Booker T. Washington reached out for help wherever he could find it. His gift for fundraising and communication, both in person and in writing, served him well. He worked with both the white and black communities, the poor and the rich, the powerful and the disenfranchised. When he first took his fundraising beyond the local community, he focused on the old abolition network still active in the Northeast. He found many people there eager and willing to support his efforts. But soon his sphere of influence and network of support reached beyond the African American

This photograph shows Booker T. Washington reading behind his office desk.

community. Washington was admired and his opinions and ideas were solicited by many wealthy and powerful men, including presidents.

The Attention of Presidents

When Booker T. Washington arrived in Tuskegee, he knew that this would be his life's work. His goals for the school went far beyond simply getting a small teaching college up and running. For Washington, the school was more than a way to improve the living conditions of the local black community. He saw the Tuskegee project as nothing less than an opportunity to change the way the nation viewed former slaves and to reduce, if not end, prejudice toward blacks. When it came to impressing his fellow Americans, he aimed high: "Soon after starting the Tuskegee Institute I earnestly desired to have the President of the United States visit it. The chance of securing such a visit seemed to be so unattainable that I dared not mention it to my nearest friend; still, I resolved that such a visit should be made." Washington also realized that if he wanted to attract the attention of the president, he had to make a big impression. At the very beginning of the school, he told both teachers and students, "We must try to perform every duty entrusted to us, not only as well, but better than anyone else, so as to receive proper consideration."[1]

Soon, he did attract the attention of presidents. Grover Cleveland, who had been a teacher before going into the law, spoke up for the college and Washington's work. Both William McKinley and Theodore Roosevelt visited the campus. However, it was not politicians as much as business magnates who became the biggest supporters, both financially and philosophically, of Tuskegee and the work that Washington did there.

Captains of Industry

In the late nineteenth century, many industries, such as steel, coal, oil, and the railroads, were booming. It was a highly competitive and innovative time in American industry. The men who owned these businesses and the bankers who funded them became extraordinarily rich. These men were often called "captains of industry." Critics dubbed them "robber barons," and the nickname stuck. This was because their business practices were often highly unethical. They fought for dominance in their industries, ruthlessly weeding out the competition and building giant monopolies. They built and protected these industrial empires by intimidation of workers and competitors, and not infrequently the use of outright violence. Their business dealings and accounting practices were also very often fraudulent. Bribes, kickbacks, and nefarious stock practices were a routine part of the way they did business. They exploited workers and took no heed for the safety of their employees, customers, or the society in which they operated. They employed children to work in dangerous jobs. While they were hoarding and protecting huge fortunes, much of the population—particularly in the South— was mired in poverty.

James Fisk became one of the richest financiers on Wall Street by smuggling and nefarious stock market practices. During the Civil War, he smuggled cotton from the Southern states to mills in the North and invested his profits in Confederate dollars. Then he sold off his Confederate currency to European investors before they knew that the Union was about to win the war and the Confederate currency would soon collapse. Jay Gould made his fortune in gold and railroads. Notorious for union busting, Gould is famous for having said, "I can hire half the working class to shoot the other half."[2]

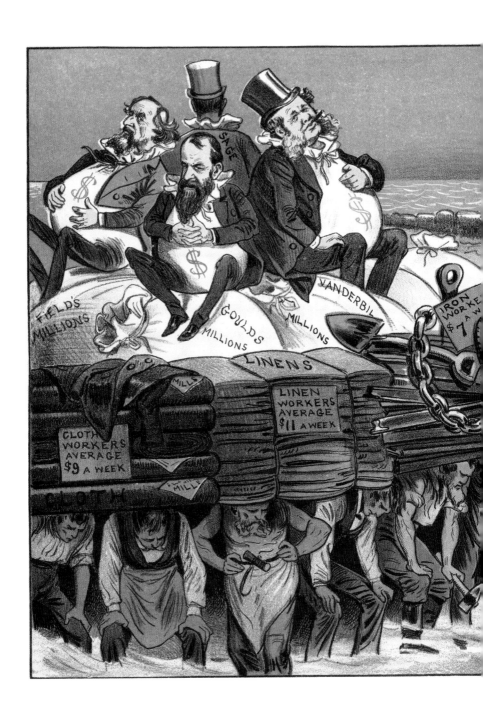

Booker T. Washington: Civil Rights Leader and Education Advocate

This political cartoon from 1883 satirizes how the wealth of business elites, such as Cyrus Field, Jay Gould, Cornelius Vanderbilt, and Russell Sage, was built on the backs of the workers.

John D. Rockefeller made his fortune in oil. He founded the Standard Oil Company in 1870 and quickly became the richest man in the world. He is often said to be America's first billionaire. Rockefeller conspired with the railroads to make sure his company dominated the delivery of oil products.

Leland Stanford, a railway magnate, became governor of California in 1862. While governor, he authorized state funds to help build a transcontinental railway—*while* he was president of the Central Pacific Railroad. He also bribed members of Congress to support his business endeavors and engaged in many other shady practices.

However, these men have come to be remembered not for their crimes and duplicity, but for their good works. For a variety of reasons, some noble, others as self-serving as their business practices, many of these robber barons turned in later years to philanthropy. Stanford and his wife, Jane, established Stanford University, a private college near Palo Alto, California, after their only son died of typhoid fever. In some cases, guilt was more of a motivation than grief, and most had their legacy in mind.

Because of their business practices, most were not well loved by the population. Charity work was a way to change that impression before the history books were written. Rockefeller devoted the last four decades of his life to charity. He generously supported many causes, including medical research, the arts, and education. Rockefeller was deeply religious, so it is possible that the philanthropy of his later years was an attempt to make up for the unethical way he earned his fortune. He was a big supporter of the Tuskegee Institute, as well as other colleges and universities for African Americans.

For others, the motivation may still have been greed. Many of these magnates were great supporters of industrial education for blacks. Some people believe the motive was to ensure a steady supply of workers for their industries.

A Gospel of Wealth

Of all the robber barons who turned to good works in their retirement years, Andrew Carnegie is probably the most well known today. Carnegie was born in Dunfermline, Scotland, in 1835. His family immigrated to the United States, settling in the Pittsburgh, Pennsylvania, area, when he was thirteen years old. His family was quite poor, and Carnegie worked at various factory jobs to help the family earn a living. He also worked hard to educate himself by reading widely on his own and attending night school after work. When he was only sixteen, he got a job as a telegraph operator, and soon after he began working for the Pennsylvania Railroad as assistant to one of the company executives.

Carnegie advanced rapidly and learned a great deal about business and industry. He invested in a variety of industries, particularly oil, and his investments were lucrative. With his profits, he founded the Carnegie Steel Company and became one of the world's wealthiest men. However, when he was still in his sixties he sold his company for a princely sum and devoted the rest of his life to philanthropy.

Unlike some captains of industry, whose philanthropy may have been motivated at least in part by guilt, Carnegie based his good works on a very particular philosophy. The Industrial Revolution had created a stark inequality of wealth in the nation. Some people, such as Carnegie himself, became incredibly rich from the manufacture of goods. Meanwhile, those who labored to produce and transport those goods worked for low wages and shared in very little of the enormous profits produced by

Andrew Carnegie (*first row, center right*) and Booker T. Washington (*first row, center left*) pose side by side in this group shot taken at Tuskegee in 1906.

these industries. They received no protections in case of injury or job loss due to layoffs by the company. If they died without savings (and few made enough money to save), their families were left without any means of support.

Carnegie's solution to this disparity was not to share the profits of industry more evenly throughout society, but to use that money to provide opportunities for those with the talents and skills to make it on their own. He did not see a problem with this lopsided accumulation of wealth. In fact, he thought it was a good thing. He outlined his approach in two articles written for the *North American Review* and republished by the Carnegie Foundation as *The Gospel of Wealth*: "Not evil, but good, has come to the race from the accumulation of wealth by those who have the ability and energy that produce it."[3] However, he did believe that the wealthy should, during their lives, use their wealth for the good of the community, rather than on lavish lifestyles. He advised the wealthy to live modestly and take care of their families. Beyond that, they should use their wealth in a way that would be most likely to benefit the community. The "man of wealth," he wrote, should be a "trustee" for the poor, using his "superior wisdom, experience, and ability to administer, doing for them better than they would or could do for themselves."[4] This was a very paternalistic attitude toward the poor—not to mention a willingness to completely abandon to their fate those who did not have the skills and talents to capitalize on his largess. However, he did believe—much like Washington—that providing education to the poor was the best way of helping them succeed.

One day while golfing, a friend shared with Carnegie some anecdotes from *Up from Slavery*. Carnegie was intrigued and read Washington's autobiography. He was impressed with how similar the two men's stories were. Both had been born extremely poor in childhood (though, of course, Carnegie was never a slave), and had overcome enormous obstacles to get an education. Their attitudes about the value of education, independence, and hard work were also quite similar. Carnegie felt a strong affinity with Washington and immediately allocated funds to build a library on the Tuskegee campus. This was just the beginning of Carnegie's generous support of the school.

ROSENWALD SCHOOLS

Not all of Washington's work nor the support he attracted went to Tuskegee, and not all his work in education was for adults.

Julius Rosenwald made his fortune in the retail catalog business, as a partner in Sears, Roebuck and Company. When Rosenwald, a Jew, first turned to philanthropy, he focused on the Jewish community. However, a race riot in his hometown of Springfield, Illinois, brought to his attention the problems of the black community.

Booker T. Washington had an idea about what Rosenwald could do to help African Americans. There was a great need for schools for black children. Washington asked Rosenwald to build six schools for black children in Alabama. Rosenwald agreed and built these schools in 1913 and 1914. He didn't stop there, however. By the time he was finished, Rosenwald had built more than five thousand schools all around the South to educate black children and prepare them to go on to higher education at schools like Tuskegee, Hampton, and others.

Rosenwald and Washington's project was innovative in that they developed the concept we now call "matching funds." Washington believed it was important for communities to invest in their own future. People in the towns where the schools were built would donate building materials and labor to help get their school up and running.

Rosenwald schools were in lovely buildings too. They were well lit with natural light and especially noted for their good sanitation and ventilation. This was a very long way from the slave cabin of Washington's childhood.

At one point, 40 percent of black children in the South attended a Rosenwald school. John Lewis and Rosa Parks, future leaders of the civil rights movement, were two people who attended these schools.

This is the Longstreet Rosenwald school in Longstreet, Louisiana. Its large, tall windows and cheery white paint offer an inviting atmosphere.

Washington and Carnegie's approach to industrial education for blacks was not merely a means of uplifting African Americans. It was an attempt to solve the nation's problem of racial bigotry. Carnegie's "gospel of wealth" was intended to heal the divisions between rich and poor, and most blacks were poor. Washington believed that "Friction between the races will pass away" when "the black man, by reason of his skill, intelligence, and character, can produce something that the white man wants or respects in the commercial world." When blacks "produce something that makes the white man partly dependent upon the negro, instead of all the dependence being on the other side,—a change takes place in the relations of the races," he wrote.[5]

Taking the Baton

Of course, Washington's support and influences did not come only from the wealthy white community. He had strong ties with black leaders as well. Until his death in 1895, Frederick Douglass was the undisputed leader of the African American community. However, Douglass and Washington had different approaches as to how aggressive African Americans should be when it came to demanding political and civil rights. Douglass began advocating for this as soon as the Civil War was won and became even more active in support of civil and political rights for blacks in his later years. He saw no reason to wait.

Washington favored a more gradual approach. However, the two great leaders agreed more than they disagreed. They were both staunch supporters of the Republican Party, had a strong work ethic, and were believers in the value of industrial education to help improve the lot of African Americans. They were both, despite the problems and setbacks they dealt with throughout their lives, very optimistic about the future of the black community.

The difference in the two men's approaches to leading their people was at least in part due to the fact that Douglass lived in the North and Washington in the South. Washington had to face the very practical and immediate effects of bigotry on a daily basis. When Douglass denounced whites for the circumstances faced by blacks, he did not have to face their immediate retaliation. Washington knew that if he wanted to accomplish anything for his school, its students, or his people, he had to work very carefully to keep from doing more harm than good.

When Douglass died, Washington seemed the natural person to succeed him. Indeed, Washington was very popular among average black citizens as well as most of the black leadership. Tuskegee was doing very well, and he was not only a well-respected advocate for industrial education, but a living example of what a black man could accomplish. However, there were a few black leaders who did not agree at all with Washington's philosophy or his practical approach.

CHAPTER FOUR

~

Work of a Lifetime

Much of Booker T. Washington's attitudes and philosophy about education and life in general can be attributed to his personal experiences. Though he spent his early childhood as a slave, it was likely his later childhood and early adulthood as an emancipated slave—what was then called a freedman—that informed his view of life and politics. His life's work was to empower his race, but he was determined to do this through education and entrepreneurship rather than political action.

This is a hand-tinted photograph of the Tuskegee campus, circa 1905.

A Serious Thing

At the end of the Civil War, the former Confederate states were in terrible shape. They had just lost a four-year war that was fought mainly on their own territory. The economy and infrastructure were in a shambles. Crops had been destroyed, and there was little industry to speak of. It was not an easy place to get by even if you had a home and a source of food and income. For recently emancipated slaves, the situation was almost impossible.

Suddenly being told that you were free after generations of being held in captivity was a wonderful thing. But it did pose some problems. Washington described the day he and the other slaves on the plantation where he lived were told they were free. They had been expecting the news. Rumors had been rampant for some time that the war was almost over and that, in the end, all slaves would be freed. Then one day all the slaves on the plantation, even children, like nine-year-old Washington, were told to come to the plantation house. When they arrived, a man Washington assumed was a United States Army officer made a speech and read something from a piece of paper, most likely the Emancipation Proclamation. After reading the paper, the officer told them that they were free and could go wherever they liked. Washington's mother cried and kissed her children. There was a great deal of joy and celebration on the plantation. However, the excitement was very soon tempered by a realization of the enormity of what lay ahead. In his autobiography, Washington describes what that felt like:

> The great responsibility of being free, of having charge of themselves, of having to think and plan for themselves and their children, seemed to take

possession of them. It was very much like suddenly turning a youth of ten or twelve years out into the world to provide for himself. In a few hours the great questions with which the Anglo-Saxon race had been grappling for centuries had been thrown upon these people to be solved. These were the questions of a home, a living, the rearing of children, education, citizenship, and the establishment and support of churches … To some it seemed that, now that they were in actual possession of it, freedom was a more serious thing than they had expected to find it.[1]

People who had lived and worked on plantations their whole lives under difficult conditions now needed to find new places to live, sources of food, and professions to make an income. The Freedmen's Bureau organized schools to teach former slaves to read, and distributed donations of food and clothing from the North. However, the question of how to provide for nearly four million people who had gained freedom but lost their homes (such as they were) and their source of support (such as it was) was an enormous challenge. In addition, Southern whites were not in great shape either, and not in much of a mood to help slaves that most of them hadn't wanted to see freed in the first place.

In his book *Sick from Freedom: African-American Illness and Suffering During the Civil War and Reconstruction*, historian Jim Downs explains that many former slaves died of illnesses, such as cholera and smallpox, or even starved to death in the years just after emancipation. Downs argues that there were several reasons for this neglect of newly freed Americans. First, he says, the people of the North weren't much more interested

Here, recently freed slaves gather in a Southern town shortly after the Civil War. Finding work and establishing homes was an enormous challenge for people.

in the welfare of blacks than were Southerners. The war had been won, the Union saved, and any guilt they might have felt about slavery (and by no means were all Northerners troubled over slavery) had been taken care of by emancipation. Abolitionists, on the other hand, may have been hesitant to admit how difficult things were for freed slaves. If they did, it could be seen as giving support to those who had advocated a more gradual approach to abolition based on the idea that freed slaves could not survive on their own.

In any case, the situation for freed slaves was complex, both politically and economically. As one freedman put it, "We colored people did not know how to be free and the white people did not know how to have a free colored person about them."[2]

A Rare and Noble Human Being

Washington was intimately familiar with these struggles. His own family walked 200 miles

(322 km) from the plantation in the Blue Ridge Mountains of Virginia to join his mother's husband in Malden, West Virginia. They made the entire journey on foot, sleeping outside and cooking their meager rations over a campfire. The trip took several weeks. They were fortunate that Jane's husband had a job in Malden, but they still lived in dire poverty. Yet poverty was not the only problem they faced. Transitioning from life in slavery to life as a free family was challenging on many levels. Washington recalls that while they were slaves, his family did not eat together—or even eat in the way free people generally do. When living on the plantation—and to some degree even after—the children got their meals in much the same way "dumb animals get theirs. It was a piece of bread here and a scrap of meat there. It was a cup of milk at one time and some potatoes at another. Sometimes a portion of our family would eat out of the skillet or pot, while some one else would eat from a tin plate held on the knees, and often using nothing but the hands with which to hold the food."[3] Because slaves were used, much like animals, to work for whites, they were often treated like animals. Slave families were given little respect. A slave owner could, and often did, break up slave families when they were bought or sold. Slaves had little opportunity to develop a strong family culture.

Washington learned many of his attitudes about African Americans and how they could best advance from his early mentor, Samuel Armstrong. Armstrong, a white man, was an officer in the Union army during the Civil War. He led two different regiments of black soldiers. Prior to this, he had had little experience with black people. Though he was an abolitionist, he had doubts about the potential of the black race. His experience working with black troops, however, convinced him that blacks were as capable as whites. Later he wrote, "My experiences convinced me of the excellent qualities and capacities of the freedmen. Their quick response to good treatment and to discipline was a constant surprise."[4]

After the war, Armstrong worked directing the federal government's Freedmen's Bureau. He was in charge of the eastern Virginia branch. Then, in 1868, he established the Hampton Normal and Agricultural Institute (now Hampton University) to train black teachers. And, of course, Booker T. Washington would be one of his best and most famous pupils. Washington described Armstrong as "the noblest, rarest human being that it has ever been my privilege to meet."[5] Armstrong returned the affection. When he recommended Washington for the job at Tuskegee, he said Washington was "the best man we ever had here."[6]

In addition to being noble, Armstrong was exceedingly practical. He did not believe in giving his students a classical education. Latin, Greek, and the history of ancient civilizations were not a part of Hampton's curriculum. However, the students were taught mathematics, biology, history, and English. English studies included grammar, composition, rhetoric, and elocution. And of course, agricultural subjects were taught.

Armstrong took a somewhat fatherly approach to his students. He sought to instill in them values such as thrift and responsibility, hard work and good character. He stressed hygiene and grooming. Today this sounds a bit insulting, but for many recently freed slaves, no one had ever had the time or inclination to teach them how to brush their teeth or wash their hair. Washington recalls that when he was issued bedsheets for his bed at Hampton, he didn't know how sheets worked. This was a young man who had spent most of his childhood sleeping on a pallet of rags. Two crisp, clean bedsheets were not only a luxury, but they were a bit of a mystery. The first night he slept

A PROUD TRADITION

In the years before and just after the Civil War, few white colleges and universities (and none in the South) would accept black students. Before the Civil War there were only a few black colleges in the North. However, after the war, many more were built in an effort to educate newly freed slaves who had not been allowed even to learn to read. Many were land grant schools. That is, the state would provide land and some funding in exchange for the school offering some kind of service—usually agricultural advice and assistance—to the local population. Land grant colleges were meant to focus on agricultural and industrial skills, though they were not prohibited from teaching classical subjects as well. The land grant program was initiated by laws and passed during Reconstruction. It required states to either allow blacks to attend their colleges or provide separate colleges for blacks.

Many of these schools, like Tuskegee, went on to become full colleges and even universities, and many of them still exist today. These are now called historically black colleges and universities (HBCUs). Howard University in Washington, DC, Morehead State University and Spelman College in Georgia, Alabama A & M University and Miles College in Alabama, Fisk University in Tennessee, and Alcorn State University in Mississippi are a few examples of well-respected HBCU's still in operation.

Tuskegee was unusual in one way. Initially most HBCUs had white leadership. Tuskegee had a black president and employed all-black faculty from the outset.

under both sheets. The second night he tried sleeping on top of both. Finally, he figured out that he was meant to sleep between the sheets. It was, he discovered, a very comfortable arrangement.

Armstrong never for a moment let his students forget that they were living in a world that was run by white people. He encouraged them to be peaceful, avoid conflict, and try to get on well with whites. In fact, he encouraged them to assimilate into white society as much as possible. However, he actively discouraged his students from getting involved in politics. He strongly believed that they needed to become economically independent and establish a stable family and community life before trying to achieve political equality. He believed that blacks would end prejudice by living in a way that would demonstrate that prejudice was wrongheaded. Washington took these same attitudes and approaches with him to Tuskegee.

A School Without a Campus

When Washington arrived at Tuskegee, he knew almost immediately that he had found his life's work. He was young and eager to put into practice and pass on to his students the lessons he had learned from Armstrong. He soon found that he had far more to overcome than the lack of land, buildings, or funding for the school.

The population of Tuskegee was predominately black, and the locals were very supportive of the school. Students were waiting for Washington when he arrived, ready to enroll and begin their studies. However, the conditions for blacks in Alabama were still not good, even sixteen years after the war had ended. They suffered even more poverty than blacks in some other parts of the South. And racism had only increased since the end of Reconstruction. In many areas around the South, the

These students attend history class at Tuskegee in 1899. Though Tuskegee did not focus on the classics, it did teach the basics of a liberal arts education, including the subject of history.

Ku Klux Klan had burned black homes and churches, and even killed people in an attempt to frighten and intimidate blacks and any whites who wanted to help them. These terrorists especially targeted black schools, which white supremacists saw as particularly threatening. Racial hatred was growing and lynchings were becoming distressingly common.

Even some whites who did not condone or support terrorism against blacks nonetheless believed that schools like Tuskegee and the work Washington was doing encouraged blacks to aspire to a place in society that was beyond their station. A white columnist wrote in the *Atlanta Constitution* that even though some blacks were "right smart" it didn't prove the need to educate blacks. "I saw an educated hog a few years ago that could play cards with his nose and tell the time of day on a watch," he wrote, "but that don't prove that we ought to educate hogs and send em to college. The masses of the negro race are never so happy as when in the cornfield or the cotton patch and being dependent upon the white man for protection and advice."[7]

It was an enormous challenge, but Washington firmly believed that if African Americans were to have any chance at all, they must be educated and develop economic independence.

Much of the work Washington did with his students was designed as a deliberate repudiation of white stereotypes about blacks. At that time many whites believed blacks were lazy, so Washington insisted his students go above and beyond any normal description of industry. Many whites believed blacks were sexually promiscuous, so Washington insisted on a strict moral code for his students. He set out to prove these ideas for the unfair stereotypes that they were. However, in order to do so, he had to make sure that his students were faultless. Any small misstep might be taken as evidence that the detractors were right.

By the end of Washington's first month teaching in Tuskegee—while he was still teaching in shacks and shanties—he had fifty students. The school grew rapidly. By 1890—not quite ten years into its history—the school enrolled almost twice as many students as the University of Alabama and a third more than the Agricultural and Mechanical College at Auburn (what would become Auburn University). By the end of Washington's life, Tuskegee would be one of the most respected black educational institutions in the nation. The success of Tuskegee was due in large part to Washington's exceptional organizational skills. However, it could not have been done without a great deal of financial support. Washington was an excellent fundraiser. His methods ranged from speaking at large gatherings to going door-to-door asking for support. However, one of the most powerful tools in his fundraising kit was his pen. Washington was an excellent writer. His style was direct and friendly. His many articles and books, including his 1901 autobiography, *Up from Slavery*, served as inspiration to a generation of African Americans. But many of Washington's writings were aimed at white people who were in a position to donate money to Tuskegee and otherwise support the work of improving the conditions of African Americans. *Up from Slavery*, in particular, explains in a very accessible way Washington's educational philosophy. It was his approach that convinced many philanthropists that his was a cause worth backing.

On Stage at the Expo

Washington's commitment to the economic success of the African American community was the driving force behind his creation of the National Negro Business League

(NNBL). It was something like a chamber of commerce for black businesses, and was intended to support and foster black entrepreneurship. The NNBL held conventions each summer, and at these meetings speakers and attendees would address the problems and potential solutions to problems faced by black business owners. Washington addressed these conventions each year, and much of his most loyal support came from NNBL members.

As Washington wrote and spoke to more and more organizations in his capacity as leader of the Tuskegee Institute, he became an important figure in black education and a recognized and respected voice for the African American community. However, Washington spoke differently when he talked with blacks than when he spoke with whites. His tone with black students and black leaders was encouraging, and he stressed their potential as a race and as individuals. With whites, he was more likely to stress reassurances that the gains being made by African Americans—the gains he was working hard to foster—should not be seen in any way as a threat to whites. This carefully designed dual message had been essential for gaining support for his work and preventing controversies that could have shut down the school. Yet it still kept the focus on the importance of educational and economic advancement for blacks.

The 1895 Cotton States Agricultural Exposition was held in Atlanta, Georgia. This was one of a series of exhibitions common in the late nineteenth century that showcased the technological advances of society. The 1895 exhibition was the most ambitious so far. Several Southern states hosted exhibits, and a special "Negro Building" was set aside (segregated from the main exposition hall) to feature the accomplishments of the African American community. Washington was asked to curate this portion of the event. He spent much of the year before working on it.

Just a month before the opening, he was asked to be one of the main speakers at the opening of the exposition. It was very unusual for a black man to be so recognized at an event such as this. It also presented something of a challenge for Washington. A white friend in Tuskegee warned him that this speech would be tricky—perhaps even something of a trap—telling Washington, "In Atlanta you will have to speak before Northern white people, Southern white people and Negroes all together. I fear they have got you into a pretty tight place."[8] But Washington was up to the task. His speech was magnificent. He spoke without notes and came from behind the podium to walk up and down the stage as he spoke. He addressed the audience in a direct, friendly style, yet used powerful techniques such as repeated phrases, strategic pauses, and figurative language to engage his listeners. It was and is considered one of the greatest examples of public speaking in United States history. It made Washington an instant celebrity.

It also created no small amount of controversy and was used to challenge his role as the heir apparent of the African American community.

CHAPTER FIVE

Hero to Some, Betrayer to Others

Washington was painfully aware of both the prejudice and violence toward his people, and the economic struggles of white Southerners. He believed that the route to reconciliation between the races was through mutual, interdependent progress for blacks and whites. He wrote and spoke widely, and his views were well known by anyone who was paying attention. However, it was not until the 1895 Cotton States Agricultural Exposition that he became a figure on the national stage.

Washington speaks to a crowd in Mound Bayou, Mississippi, in 1912. He had a natural speaking style that easily engaged his audiences.

The Atlanta Compromise

September 18, 1895, was a very hot day in Atlanta, Georgia. Nevertheless, thousands of people attended the Cotton States Expo. Military units paraded down Peachtree Street while bands played. Politicians, diplomats, business leaders, and many ordinary citizens came out to see a showcasing of the industry and technology that had replaced the plantation economy of the South. Sectional differences were on display as well. The crowd cheered when the band played "The Star-Spangled Banner." When the band played "Dixie," the unofficial theme song of the South, cheers erupted into a roar. When it played "Yankee Doodle," the crowd settled back down.

When Washington took the stage in the Gilbert Auditorium that day, it was the first time a black speaker had addressed a mixed-race audience in the South. Blacks were confined to a separate seating area, but they *were* welcomed inside. For Atlanta in 1895, that was a big deal. If Washington was walking a fine line here, so were the event's organizers.

Washington had to convince whites that black people were as capable and deserving as white people. And he had to do this without appearing threatening to whites, which might have the opposite effect from what he sought. At the same time, the organization's sponsors had to convince the nation (and especially its investors and bankers) that Atlanta, a city aiming to be the capital of the New South, was not riven by racial hatred and violence. They had a lot riding on Booker T. Washington. And he delivered.

Washington began by thanking the event's organizers for recognizing the black race, which, he pointed out, made up one-third of the population of the South. Then he all but apologized for the early years of Reconstruction when blacks sought political office and the power of the vote. It was understandable, he said, that to the newly freed slave, "a seat in Congress or the State Legislature was more sought than real-estate or industrial skill, that the political convention, or stump speaking" was more attractive than "starting a dairy farm or truck garden." While never denying the capability of blacks to handle political power or the fact that they deserved it, he effectively admitted that it had been a mistake for them to try to achieve it so soon after emancipation. The first priority of the black community was and should be, he told the crowd that day, to achieve economic independence. "It is important and right that all privileges of the law be ours, but it is vastly more important that we be prepared for the exercise of these privileges," he said.[1]

Washington also addressed, if subtly, the idea that blacks should leave the South for the North, or even for another country. Many white nationalists, and even a few abolitionists before the war, had suggested plans for setting up colonies of freed slaves in Africa. Some blacks had embraced this idea. Others favored moving North where there was more industrial opportunity, and possibly less racial hatred. In his speech, Washington told the story of a ship that had been lost at sea for many days. The passengers were out of fresh water and dying of thirst. They came upon another vessel and signaled them, asking for water. The ship responded, "Cast down your bucket where you are," for the lost ship had strayed upriver into fresh water.[2] Washington used this metaphor—and repeated the phrase "cast down your bucket"—to remind his people of two things. First, to work with what they had: farming and industry first, political power later. And second, to stay put. They belonged in the South and were there to stay. Washington did not openly state this, but he was clearly aware

TUSKEGEE'S GENTLE ECCENTRIC

Other than Booker T. Washington, the most celebrated person at Tuskegee was undoubtedly George Washington Carver. In 1896, Washington hired Carver to head Tuskegee's agricultural department, and Carver did amazing things.

Carver, too, was born a slave. He, his brother, and his mother were the only slaves owned by a Missouri farming couple, Susan and Moses Carver. When George was still young, his mother disappeared and was never found. It was assumed that she had been kidnapped by slave traders. After abolition, the Carvers raised George and his brother as their own children.

Carver could not attend the local school because he was black. So when he was still young, he traveled around the Midwest working in laundries and as a cook, trying to get as much education as he could here and there. In 1890, he enrolled in Simpson College in Iowa. Carver was a very talented artist and majored in art at Simpson. He was also gifted in horticulture. After Simpson, he got a master's degree in agriculture at Iowa State College. It was there Washington found him and recruited him for Tuskegee.

Carver was brilliant—but eccentric. He developed the agricultural station at Tuskegee and was responsible for too many innovations in agriculture and industry to list. He developed paints and paper and other useful items using the local clay. He taught local farmers how to grow nutritious crops (rather than just cotton) using techniques that are the mainstays of the modern organic gardening movement, such as companion planting and crop rotation. He developed many uses for the peanut—a prolific crop in the South—so many, in fact, that he was often known as the "Peanut Man." He also continued to paint and collect butterflies. In 1941, *Time* magazine did a cover story on him, calling him the black Leonardo.

Carver was gentle and kind, but lousy at administration. He wore sloppy clothes and often refused to accept money for this scientific work. He was a religious man, and he taught Bible classes by acting out the parts of characters from Bible stories. He and Washington often argued about administrative details, but there was no doubt that Dr. Carver was one of Tuskegee's most accomplished teachers.

George Washington Carver was a great scientist and teacher, and one of Tuskegee's most distinguished faculty members. This portrait was taken around 1915.

that conditions for blacks in the North were rapidly worsening. Emigrating would likely do little good and would have the unintended effect of spreading out the black population and weakening their solidarity.

He also used the "cast down your bucket" metaphor to admonish whites to take advantage of the opportunity to hire skilled black workers. Never a fan of organized labor, Washington played on fears of unions to make his case. He urged his white listeners to cast their buckets "down among these people who have without strikes and labor wars tilled your fields, cleared your forests, [built] your railroads and cities, and … helped make possible this magnificent representation of the progress of the South." If they did, he promised his white listeners that:

> You can be sure in the future, as you have been in the past, that you and your families will be surrounded by the most patient, faithful, law-abiding and unresentful people that the world has seen. As we have proven our loyalty to you in the past, in nursing your children, watching by the sick bed of your mothers and fathers, and often following them with tear dimmed eyes to their graves, so in the future in our humble way, we shall stand by you with a devotion that no foreigner can approach, ready to lay down our lives, if need be, in defense of yours, interlacing our industrial, commercial, civil and religious life with yours in a way that shall make the interests of both races one. In all things that are purely social we can be as separate as the fingers, yet one as the hand in all things essential to mutual progress.[3]

Mixed Reviews

To today's ears that sounds like one of the most shockingly "Uncle Tom" speeches ever given. But few people heard it that way in 1895. Washington was trying to defuse increasing racial tensions by soothing the anxieties of whites. Despite the many accomplishments on display in the Negro Building, things were, in fact, getting worse for blacks, both in the South and in the North. If Washington could reverse that trend, or even stop its momentum, it would buy time for blacks to establish the economic foundation that he saw as essential to—and that must come prior to—their political success.

The speech was a rousing success. Hats and handkerchiefs were thrown in the air; women tossed flowers onto the stage. Washington was widely praised by the national press and political and business leaders. James Creelman, a journalist for the *New York World*, described the speech in the next day's paper. He wrote that none of the world's greatest orators "could have pleaded a cause with more consummate power than did this angular Negro, standing in a nimbus of sunshine, surrounded by the men who once fought to keep his race in bondage." President Grover Cleveland wrote to Washington, saying, perhaps somewhat ambiguously, "Your words cannot fail to delight and encourage all who wish well for your race."[4]

It wasn't only whites who praised the speech. A black lawyer in Chicago responded by saying that, "no word uttered by a colored man during the past twenty years will go farther and do more to set us right in public opinion."[5] In fact, most blacks were by this time of a similar opinion as to the best path forward for blacks. Washington's message of putting education and economic progress ahead of political empowerment was not a radical call for change, but a careful articulation of the approach most blacks had come to favor.

Frederick Douglass, an accepted leader of African Americans, had died just a few months before Washington's Atlanta speech, and the black community was casting around for a new leader. Douglass's shoes were indeed big ones to fill. He had been a leader in the abolitionist movement and a strong voice for the rights of former slaves after the war. Washington's newfound national fame as well as his obvious gifts for oratory and organization made him seem like the perfect candidate.

Timothy Thomas Fortune, an African American writer, newspaper publisher, and civil rights leader, was one of the most influential black public intellectuals of the period. After the Atlanta speech, Fortune immediately called for Washington to step up and be the next Frederick Douglass. He insisted that Washington's speech had with one blow reversed the common belief of the white man that African Americans were feeble minded, lacking in morals, and incapable of independence. While the speech had certainly not done quite that, it had made a huge impression on a great number of white people. Fortune's boosting of it helped it to influence considerably more.

Not all black leaders agreed, however. A few saw Washington's speech as giving ammunition to whites who wanted to make sure blacks never attained anything close to civil rights and political equality. It was labeled as "accommodationist" and dubbed "the Atlanta Compromise." Washington was, in the view of some, trading the dignity and constitutional rights of black people for the right to work for them. AME Bishop Henry McNeal Turner, a missionary and politician, said that Washington "will have to live a long time to undo the harm he has done to our race."[6] Soon, however, Washington was to get what was perhaps the harshest and

Timothy Thomas Fortune was an African American writer, newspaper publisher, and editor. He was a strong proponent of civil rights for blacks.

most lasting criticism of his leadership. It came from another black educator and the only serious rival to Washington's claim as successor to Douglass, William Edward Burghardt Du Bois.

Different Worlds

W. E. B. Du Bois was born in Massachusetts in 1868, three years after the end of the Civil War. He was valedictorian of his high school class and graduated from Fisk University in Nashville, Tennessee, in 1888. He studied at the University of Berlin in Germany and was the first African American to earn a PhD from Harvard University. His doctoral dissertation, *The Suppression of the African Slave Trade in America*, was published by Harvard University Press. His scholarly work centered on the conditions of life for African Americans in urban locations. His civil rights work focused on gaining political rights and social equality for blacks. He was one of the founders of the National Association for the Advancement of Colored People (NAACP). Unlike Washington, he was completely uncompromising on the issue of race. However, in one way, he was very much like Washington. He strongly believed that education and scholarship were the means to racial equality.

In 1894, Washington had offered Du Bois a teaching position at Tuskegee. Du Bois turned down the offer in favor of another he had received, but the two men corresponded from time to time after that. Indeed, Du Bois wrote Washington a letter complimenting him on the Atlanta address. However, it was not long before his compliments turned to criticism. In 1901, Du Bois wrote an essay about black leadership that clearly outlined his disagreements with Washington (and other black leaders). He wrote that Washington's "programme of industrial education, conciliation of the South, and submission and silence as to political and civil rights" had become not a "by-path" but a "veritable way of life."[7]

It is easy to see why the two men did not see eye-to-eye on social issues. They came from very different backgrounds

W. E. B. Du Bois, circa 1918. He was one of America's greatest intellectuals and supporters of civil rights for African Americans.

and perspectives. Washington was born in slavery and grew up in extreme poverty. While the Du Bois family was poor, they were a stable family in a good community where blacks were generally respected—not treated as no better than a cart horse or a milk cow. Du Bois went to good schools all his life. Though the Hampton Normal and Agricultural Institute was an excellent training school for teachers, it was no Harvard. Du Bois was far better educated than Washington. Some of Du Bois's harshest objections to Washington's approach, in fact, had to do with Washington's belief that blacks should be taught occupational skills before they were given a liberal arts education.

In *Up from Slavery*, Washington describes traveling around Tuskegee in the first month after he arrived there. The poverty he encountered was shocking, and he found that many of the people (though by no means all) who lived there had few or no skills for making a living, and no real notion of how to go about keeping house or planting food on the small plots of land they lived on. Washington writes:

> The common diet of the people was fat pork and corn bread. At times I have eaten in cabins where they had only corn bread and "black-eye peas" cooked in plain water. The people seemed to have no other idea than to live on this fat meat and corn bread,—the meat, and the meal of which the bread was made, having been bought at a high price at a store in town, notwithstanding the fact that the land all about the cabin homes could easily have been made to produce nearly every kind of garden vegetable that is raised anywhere in the country … I remember that on one occasion when I went into

one of these cabins for dinner, when I sat down to the table for a meal with the four members of the family, I noticed that, while there were five of us at the table, there was but one fork for the five of us to use.[8]

No doubt this was a kind of poverty that Du Bois may have been aware of but could probably not truly understand. However, it was Washington's answer to this problem that seemed to most irk Du Bois.

In another passage in *Up from Slavery*, Washington says that "one of the saddest things I saw … was a young man, who had attended some high school, sitting down in a one-room cabin, with grease on his clothing, filth all around him, and weeds in the yard and garden, engaged in studying a French grammar."[9] Washington certainly saw the value of learning French—or any other foreign language. Likewise, he no doubt appreciated the industry of a student who would sit down in the midst of chaos to devote himself to his studies. However, what was clear to Washington but not obvious to Du Bois was that these incredibly poor people desperately needed financial security and social dignity if they were to survive among Southern whites. He thought learning to conjugate French verbs could wait.

Where Du Bois was basing his approach on the capacities of black people generally, Washington was working with incredibly poor people, and poor people in a region where their white neighbors cared little to nothing about their welfare. In fact, all too often they lived in fear for their lives at the hands of racist whites. What Washington called the "uplift" of blacks was, in his world, a matter of life and death. He passionately believed that economic independence was

W. E. B. Du Bois (*standing, second from right*) appears in the headquarters of the *Crisis* newspaper, circa 1932.

essential if his people were to have any hope of social and political power. He also knew that getting along with whites was necessary to their survival.

As Washington saw it, once white people came to realize the value of black people and depended on them as a vital part of the economy, then blacks could press for political equality. In his Atlanta address, Washington basically said that African Americans should be willing for the time being to accept discrimination and remain socially as separate from whites "as the fingers," as he put it. Du Bois was having no part of it.

Despite the compassionate and heartrending descriptions of the struggles of these people in *Up from Slavery*, to Du Bois, the book sounded very much like it was making the case that blacks were to be treated like children. It seemed to him that Washington was saying exactly what white people wanted to hear. It offended him deeply. He was aware, of course, that many blacks lacked the education and opportunities necessary for political success. However, he believed that focusing on those blacks who did have those advantages was the answer. Du Bois called these people "the talented tenth." He wrote, "The Negro race, like all races, is going to be saved by its exceptional men. The problem of education, then, among Negroes must first of all deal with the Talented Tenth; it is the problem of developing the Best of this race that they may guide the Mass away from the contamination and death of the Worse, in their own and other races."[10]

This disagreement between the two great black leaders would frame the debate about how best to achieve equality for blacks up until the civil rights movement.

CHAPTER SIX

Looking Back

Washington's reputation has waxed and waned over the years, but as an inspiration for using education to overcome circumstances, his legacy is still strong. Yet, even today, scholars debate whether Washington should be regarded as an Uncle Tom or a true African American hero.

A Purely Business Standpoint

Understanding Booker T. Washington requires a historical perspective as well as an appreciation for the careful path he took between standing up for his people and protecting them from the resentments and hatreds of

African American sculptor and member of the Harlem Renaissance movement Selma Burke poses with her bust of Booker T. Washington, circa 1935.

white racists. A story told by Robert Norrell in his biography of Washington demonstrates the subtleties of Washington's approach to rights for African Americans. It was 1885 and a few staff members from the Tuskegee Institute were traveling by train to Montgomery, Alabama, a journey of about 40 miles (64 km), to celebrate a wedding. They bought first-class tickets for the trip. They were all light-skinned and could pass for whites and were seated in the first-class compartment, in accordance with the tickets they had paid for. When the train stopped to refuel just outside Tuskegee, a mob of white men surrounded the train. One of the whites shouted, "There are three coons in the first class car." At that time the word "coon" was a common derogatory name for African Americans. The mob forced them off the train at gunpoint and threatened to kill them if they tried to ride any further in the first-class car. They reboarded the train in the second-class car. A few miles down the road, however, the bride and groom were arrested and fined on what Norrell calls a "spurious charge." The group decided to give up train travel, and hired horses to take them back to Tuskegee.[1]

In the South at this time, incidents like this were far from uncommon. Though blacks could buy a first-class train ticket (that would soon change), they were usually not seated in the first-class compartment. The accommodations for black people were often filthy. If a drunk or disheveled white person were to board the train, he was generally seated in the section where blacks were seated. Train travel was such an ordeal for blacks that even those who could afford the fare rarely traveled by train if there was another option.

When Washington heard about the treatment of his colleagues, he decided to speak up. He wrote a letter to the editor of the Montgomery *Advertiser*. The way he expressed his complaint is a perfect example of his approach to racial matters. He made it clear that he was not asking for "social equality or anything bordering on it." Instead, his argument was "from a purely business standpoint," he wrote. "To the negro it is a matter of dollars and cents. I claim that the railroads in Alabama do not provide as good accommodations for the colored passengers as those furnished white passengers for the same money and that the fare is not first class as claimed on the face of the ticket." He explained that meeting his request would not harm, but would in fact benefit the railroad. "This unjust practice toward the negro cuts thousands of dollars' worth of negro travel every year, while just treatment of the negro would stop no white travel."[2] He made it clear that he did not aspire to social equality for blacks. He did, however, *demand* economic equality. It was in some ways a clever, almost sneaky, approach, and it was the backbone of his method. That single sentence in a letter to the editor of a newspaper encapsulates Washington's belief in how equality and justice for blacks could and would be achieved. He thought that if African Americans could make themselves indispensable to the white economy, and make their economy interdependent with that of whites, it would eventually become clear that discrimination was not in anyone's interests.

A Bus This Time

In 1955, a boycott of public buses by African Americans led to the reversal of the Supreme Court ruling that legalized segregation by allowing "separate but equal" facilities for blacks—the foundation for the Jim Crow laws. The boycott took place in Montgomery, Alabama, the same city where Washington had sent his letter to the editor many years before.

Bus travel and virtually all aspects of public life were segregated in the South until the 1960s. This image was taken at a bus station in Durham, North Carolina, in 1940.

The Montgomery Bus Boycott is considered the beginning of the modern civil rights movement. The civil rights movement took just the opposite approach from Washington's. Civil rights leaders were most definitely *demanding* equal social and political rights for blacks. But interestingly, the boycott of the city's buses was meant to make an economic impact on the city. When blacks stopped riding the buses, the city lost a great deal of money. The technique of boycotting businesses that discriminated against blacks was frequently used by civil rights activists in the 1950s and 1960s. Though in the end, boycotts were not enough to reverse decades of discrimination against blacks, the method of economic pressure was a key part of the ongoing demand for rights for blacks.

It was during the civil rights movement that Washington's reputation began to suffer among ordinary blacks as well as among black intellectuals. This is somewhat ironic, because Washington's work on behalf of education for African Americans led the way for many blacks to become business owners, teachers, lawyers, and others who would step up and lead the movement. Martin Luther King Jr. himself got his undergraduate degree at Morehouse College in Atlanta, a historically black educational institution. We also know now that Washington quietly gave money to the NAACP and other groups that were politically active in the cause of civil rights for blacks.

Though the emphasis at Tuskegee was on industrial education, it is important to remember that Tuskegee's aim was not to prepare its students to work for whites (despite the impression Washington gave in his Atlanta address). It was to train black teachers and black entrepreneurs. Though Du Bois and others would often accuse Washington of saying that blacks should not receive higher or liberal arts education, he

In the 1950s, black people boycotted buses and walked to work in Montgomery, Alabama, to put pressure on the city to desegregate the city's buses. These people walk to work in 1956, three months into the boycott.

never said that. What he did say was that such an education would be useless without economic security, and that economic security required a different kind of training. Washington's goal was to create a class of black businesspeople and black teachers that would not only prove the economic and social value of the race but spread it to other African Americans and on to the next generation. And that is, in fact, what he did. If black intellectuals like Du Bois didn't get this, most ordinary black people certainly did.

WASHINGTON AND KING

Booker T. Washington and Martin Luther King Jr. are often thought of as polar opposites. In many ways, that was true. Washington urged African Americans to bide their time, to put up with segregation and discrimination until they had achieved educational and economic parity. King, on the other hand, led people in marches in the street demanding political and social equality.

In one of the most powerful and moving documents in US history, "Letter from a Birmingham Jail," King addressed critics who said that blacks should be patient and wait for justice and that the political actions King led were "unwise and untimely." King wrote, "We know through painful experience that freedom is never voluntarily given by the oppressor; it must be demanded by the oppressed ... For years now I have heard the word 'Wait!' It rings in the ear of every Negro with piercing familiarity. This 'Wait' has almost always meant 'Never.'"[3]

If Washington had known how long blacks would have to wait for justice and how hard they would have to work to achieve it, he may not have been so willing to compromise with whites. We can never know. But we do know that his work in educating African Americans and helping them get on their feet after emancipation paved the way for the civil rights movement to come later. Without the educational and economic support and training Washington gave his fellow African Americans, the civil rights movement might never have happened.

Martin Luther King Jr. (*at podium*) addresses a meeting of activists planning the Montgomery Bus Boycott of 1955.

However, Du Bois and others were not mistaken when they claimed that Washington was willing to accept a great deal of injustice along the way to reaching his goals. When read in the light of today's post–civil rights world, some of Washington's statements can seem galling (particularly the parts of the Atlanta speech that seem to offer the services of blacks to whites). When Washington died in 1915, Du Bois wrote a eulogy that unsparingly expressed his feelings about Washington. He wrote that blacks should be deeply grateful to Washington for his help in "the accumulation of Negro land and property, his establishment of Tuskegee and spreading of industrial education and his compelling of the white south to at least think of the Negro as a possible man." However, Du Bois went on to say that the soul of Booker T. Washington bore a "heavy responsibility for the consummation of Negro disfranchisement … and the firmer establishment of the color caste in this land."[4]

So today we are left with the question: Was Booker T. Washington an African American hero? Did he sell out his race or uplift it? Historians continue to debate the question, but in recent years more have come to see Washington as a hero rather than a sell-out. While we may wish things could have been different and change could have come faster, it is clear that Washington was doing the best he could for his people at the time and under the constraints he faced. Washington was, in all things, a pragmatist. Like King, Booker T. Washington had a dream, but it would be many years and take another dreamer to bring that dream to reality. Washington's work, however, most certainly laid the groundwork for it.

The legacy of Booker T. Washington is one of dedication to the empowerment and education of all African Americans. This photograph of Washington was taken in 1904.

CHRONOLOGY

1856 Booker Taliaferro Washington is born in Franklin County, Virginia.

1865 The Civil War ends, and Washington and his family are freed.

1872 Washington enrolls in Hampton Normal and Agricultural Institute.

1875 Washington graduates with honors from Hampton, then returns to Malden to teach school.

1881 Washington opens Tuskegee Normal and Industrial Institute.

1882 Washington marries his first wife, Fannie Norton Smith.

1883 Washington's daughter, Portia, is born.

1884 Fannie dies.

1885 Washington marries Olivia Davidson.

1887 Washington's son Booker Taliaferro Washington Jr. is born (he was named Baker Taliaferro at birth, but later changed his name).

1889 Washington's son Ernest Davidson Washington is born. Olivia dies.

1893 Washington marries Margaret Murray.

1895 Washington delivers an address at the opening of the Cotton States and International Exhibition in Atlanta, Georgia, a speech dubbed "the Atlanta Compromise" by its critics.

1898 President William McKinley visits Tuskegee Institute.

1900 Washington organizes the National Negro Business League.

1901 *Up from Slavery* is published.

1903 Andrew Carnegie gives Tuskegee Institute $600,000 in steel bonds.

1905 President Theodore Roosevelt visits Tuskegee.

1909 The National Association for the Advancement of Colored People (NAACP) is founded.

1915 Washington dies at home in Tuskegee.

GLOSSARY

accommodating Allowing or making room for the wishes and needs of a particular person or group.

appropriate To designate something for a particular use.

aristocracy The upper class in a society, usually in that position due to inherited wealth.

assimilate To blend in with a culture and adopt the practices of the culture or population.

caste A social hierarchy based on hereditary conditions such as class or race.

curate To select and organize materials and exhibits in a museum or similar display.

delegate A person who acts on behalf of others at a meeting or convention.

disenfranchise To take away or deny the right to vote.

elocution The art of clear and effective public speaking, with an emphasis on pronunciation and articulation.

emancipation Liberation, particularly the freeing of someone from slavery.

entrepreneurship The process or habit of creating one or more new businesses.

eulogy Words written or spoken on the occasion of someone's death.

fraudulent Business practices or dealings that involve criminal deceit.

inaugural Relating to the ceremony that officially begins the term of office of an official, such as a president.

infrastructure Buildings, roads, bridges, and other public works necessary for operating a society.

largess Generosity, particularly of money.

legacy Something left, such as property or money, but also reputation, after one dies.

liberal arts Literature, philosophy, history, social sciences, and other academic subjects, as opposed to subjects designed to prepare a student for a particular job or profession.

lucrative Very profitable.

lynch Murder by mob, usually by hanging.

magnate A person who has achieved great success and wealth in business.

monopoly A business or industry that has total control over a particular service or product.

naturalize To become a citizen of another country.

normal Describing a school that trains teachers.

paternalistic Treating others the way a father might treat his children, giving them little freedom and making decisions on their behalf, based on what those in power think is best for them.

philanthropist Someone who donates money or otherwise supports causes that benefit others.

platform In politics, the statement of positions or policies of a given party or candidate.

pragmatist Someone who focuses on practical rather than idealistic solutions to problems.

ratify To officially agree to or sign off on, such as an amendment or treaty.

recitation The practice of repeating out loud from memory something one is learning or has learned. Once a common educational practice.

rhetoric The art of speaking or writing in such a way as to convince or persuade.

secede To withdraw from membership in a political (or religious) alliance or federation.

succeed To inherit or take over a position of leadership upon the retirement or death of another.

supremacist Someone who believes that one group of people is superior to other groups.

Uncle Tom A black person (or used as an adjective, an action or statement) that is servile, docile, or compliant.

unethical Immoral.

SOURCES

CHAPTER ONE

1. Abraham Lincoln, "The Emancipation Proclamation," January 1, 1863 (National Archives and Records Administration, 100 Milestone Documents), https://www.ourdocuments.gov/doc.php?flash=true&doc=34&page=transcript.

2. Abraham Lincoln, "Second Annual Message," December 1, 1862, The American Presidency Project, http://www.presidency.ucsb.edu/ws/?pid=29503

3. Abraham Lincoln, "Second Inaugural Address," March 4, 1865, US National Archives and Records Administration, https://www.ourdocuments.gov/print_friendly.php?-flash=true&page=&doc=38&title=President+Abraham+Lincolns+Second+Inaugural+Address+%281865%293.

4. Robert J. Norrell, *Up from History: The Life of Booker T. Washington* (Cambridge, MA: Belknap, 2009), 162.

5. Ibid., 116–117.

6. Ibid., 117.

CHAPTER TWO

1. Booker T. Washington, *Up from Slavery*, edited with an introduction by William L. Andrews (Oxford, UK: Oxford University Press, 1995), 4.

2. Ibid., 4.

3. Ibid., 20.

4. Ibid., 21.

5. Ibid., 26.

6. Ibid., 30.

7. Ibid., 30–31.

8. Booker T. Washington, "Don't Be Discouraged," *Character Building: A Collection of His Sunday Evening Talks to the Students and Faculty at Tuskegee*, Booker T. Washington Society, http://www.btwsociety.org/library/books/Character_Building/07.php.

CHAPTER THREE

1. Booker T. Washington, *Story of My Life and Work: An Autobiography* (Toronto, Ontario, Canada: J. L. Nichols and Company, 1901), 239, from the University of North Carolina at Chapel Hill Collection "Documenting the American South," 1999, http://www.btwsociety.org/library/books/Story_of_My_Life/16.php.

2. Philip Dray, *There Is Power in a Union: The Epic Story of Labor in America* (New York: Doubleday, 2010), 124.

3. Andrew Carnegie, "The Gospel of Wealth," (New York: Carnegie Corporation, 2017), 5, https://www.carnegie.org/media/filer_public/0a/e1/0ae166c5-fca3-4adf-82a7-74c0534cd8de/gospel_of_wealth_2017.pdf.

4. Ibid., 12.

5. Booker T. Washington, "The Awakening of the Negro," (*Atlantic*, September 1896), https://www.theatlantic.com/magazine/archive/1896/09/the-awakening-of-the-negro/305449.

CHAPTER FOUR

1. Washington, *Up from Slavery*, 12–13.

2. Library of Congress, "Reconstruction and Its Aftermath," (*African American Odyssey: Part One*, United States Library of Congress), https://memory.loc.gov/ammem/aaohtml/ exhibit/aopart5.html.

3. Washington, *Up from Slavery*, 5–6.

4. Hampton Institute, *Twenty-Two Years Work at the Hampton Institute at Hampton, Virginia* (United States Library of Congress, 1893), https://archive.org/details/ twentytwoyearswo00hamp.

5. Washington, *Up from Slavery*, 32.

6. Norrell, 40.

7. Ibid., 57.

8. Bernice Tell, "Separate but One: Booker T. Washington's 'Atlanta Compromise' Displayed at Library," (*Library of Congress Information Bulletin*, February 19, 1996), https:// www.loc.gov/loc/lcib/9603/booker.html.

CHAPTER FIVE

1. Booker T. Washington, "Address at the Opening of the International Cotton States Exposition," Atlanta, Georgia, September 18, 1895.

2. Ibid.

3. Ibid.

4. "African American Perspectives, Progress of a People," (Library of Congress, Pamphlets from the Daniel A. P. Murray Collection, 1818–1907), https://memory.loc.gov/ammem/aap/aapaddr.html.

5. Norrell, 128.

6. National Park Service, "National Response to the Atlanta Address," (*National Park Service*, "Booker T. Washington Monument, Virginia"), https://www.nps.gov/bowa/learn/historyculture/in-black-and-white.htm.

7. W. E. B. Du Bois, *The Souls of Black Folk*, edited by Henry Louis Gates, Jr. and Terri Hume Oliver (New York: Norton, 1999), 34.

8. Washington, *Up from Slavery*, 65–66.

9. Ibid., 71.

10. W. E. B. Du Bois, "The Talented Tenth," in *The Negro Problem: A Series of Articles by Representative Negroes of Today* (University of California Berkeley archives, full text online), page 33, https://archive.org/stream/negroproblemseri00washrich/negroproblemseri00washrich_djvu.txt.

CHAPTER SIX

1. Norrell, 79.

2. Cary D. Wintz, ed., *African American Political Thought, 1890–1930: Washington, Du Bois, Garvey, and Randolph* (London, UK: Routledge, 2015), 21.

3. Martin Luther King Jr., "Letter from a Birmingham Jail," April 16, 1963, *The King Encyclopedia*, Stanford University, http://kingencyclopedia.stanford.edu/encyclopedia/documentsentry/annotated_letter_from_birmingham/index.html.

4. Du Bois, *Souls of Black Folk*, 171.

FURTHER INFORMATION

BOOKS

Bailey, Budd. *Booker T. Washington and the Tuskegee Institute.* New York: Cavendish Square, 2017.

Cunningham, Meghan Engsberg. *W. E. B. Du Bois: Co-Founder of the NAACP.* New York: Cavendish Square, 2017.

Foner, Eric. *A Short History of Reconstruction.* New York: Harper Perennial, 2015.

Lovett, Bobby L. *America's Historically Black Colleges and Universities: A Narrative History, 1837–2009.* Macon, GA: Mercer University Press, 2015.

Washington, Booker T. *Up from Slavery*, edited with an introduction by William L. Andrews. Oxford, UK: Oxford University Press, 1995.

WEBSITES

Booker T. Washington Society
http://www.btwsociety.org/library

This site contains a wealth of Washington's writings, including speeches, letters, articles, books, and the weekly talks he gave to Tuskegee students on Sunday evenings.

Library of Congress American Memory Collection
https://memory.loc.gov/ammem/aap/booker.wav

This is a link to an audio recording of Booker T. Washington's speech at the Atlanta Expo.

NAACP
https://www.naacp.org/

This website is the official page of the National Association for the Advancement of Colored People, which Booker T. Washington's critic W. E. B. Du Bois helped start.

Tuskegee University
https://www.tuskegee.edu/

Visit the website of Tuskegee University, the name by which the Tuskegee Institute is known today. Based in Tuskegee, Alabamab, it continues to be a place celebrating education for all.

US Department of Education/Office for
Civil Rights: Historically Black Colleges and
Universities and College Desegregation
https://www2.ed.gov/about/offices/list/ocr/docs/hq9511.html

History, background, and other information regarding HBCUs and desegregation of colleges, including links to financial aid information.

MUSEUMS

National Museum of African American
History and Culture
1400 Constitution Ave. NW
Washington, DC 20560

National Park Service Booker T. Washington
National Monument Virginia
12130 Booker T. Washington Highway
Hardy, VA 24101

National Park Service Tuskegee Institute
National Historic Site Alabama
1212 West Montgomery Road
Tuskegee Institute, AL 36088

BIBLIOGRAPHY

Carnegie, Andrew. "The Gospel of Wealth," New York: Carnegie Corporation, 2017. https://www.carnegie.org/media/filer_public/0a/e1/0ae166c5-fca3-4adf-82a7-74c0534cd8de/gospel_of_wealth_2017.pdf.

Carroll, Rebecca, ed. *Uncle Tom or New Negro?: African Americans Reflect on Booker T. Washington and Up From Slavery 100 Years Later.* New York: Broadway Books, 2006.

Coates, Ta-Nehisi. "The Tragedy and Betrayal of Booker T. Washington." *Atlantic*, March 31, 2009. https://www.theatlantic.com/entertainment/archive/2009/03/the-tragedy-and-betrayal-of-booker-t-washington/7092.

———. *We Were Eight Years in Power: An American Tragedy.* New York: One World, 2017.

Downs, Jim. *Sick from Freedom: African-American Illness and Suffering During the Civil War and Reconstruction.* Oxford, UK: Oxford University Press, 2012.

Dray, Philip. *At the Hands of Persons Unknown: The Lynching of Black America.* New York: Modern Library, 2002.

———. Capitol Men: *The Epic Story of the First Black Congressmen.* Boston, MA: Houghton Mifflin, 2008.

———. *There Is Power in a Union: The Epic Story of Labor in America*. New York: Doubleday, 2010.

Du Bois, W.E. B. *Against Racism: Unpublished Essays, Papers, Addresses, 1887–1961*. Amherst, MA: University of Massachusetts Press, 1985.

———. *Black Folk Then and Now*. Oxford, UK: Oxford University Press, 2007.

———. *The Souls of Black Folk*, edited by Henry Louis Gates, Jr. and Terri Hume Oliver. New York: Norton, 1999.

Foner, Eric. *Forever Free: The Story of Emancipation and Reconstruction*. New York: Vintage, 2005.

———. *A Short History of Reconstruction*. New York: Harper Perennial, 2015.

Hampton Institute. *Twenty-Two Years Work at the Hampton Institute at Hampton, Virginia*. United States Library of Congress, 1893. https://archive.org/details/twentytwoyearswo00hamp

Jean-Laurent, Annabella. "Flashback: The 1895 Cotton States Exposition and the Negro Building." *Atlanta Magazine*, February 27, 2014. http://www.atlantamagazine.com/news-culture-articles/flashback-the-1895-cotton-states-exposition-and-the-negro-building.

King, Martin Luther Jr. *The Radical King*, edited and introduced by Cornel West. Boston, MA: Beacon, 2015.

Library of Congress. "Reconstruction and Its Aftermath," *African American Odyssey: Part One*, US Library of Congress. https://memory.loc.gov/ammem/aaohtml/exhibit/aopart5.html.

Lubin, Gus, et al. "Meet the 24 Robber Barons Who Once Ruled America." *Business Insider*, March 20, 2012. http://www.businessinsider.com/americas-robber-barons-2012-3?op=1.

McClure, Brian. "Booker T. Washington, Andrew Carnegie, and a Gift for a Lifetime." May 11, 2011. *State of HBCUS, Past, Present and Future*. https://stateofhbcus.wordpress.com/2011/05/11/booker-t-washington-andrew-carnegie-and-a-gift-for-a-lifetime.

McPherson, James. *Battle Cry of Freedom: The Civil War Era*. New York: Oxford University Press, 1988.

National Park Service. "Tuskegee Institute National Historic Site, Tuskegee, Alabama." https://www.nps.gov/nr/travel/cultural_diversity/tuskegee_institute_national_historic_site.html.

Norrell, Robert J. *Up from History: The Life of Booker T. Washington*. Cambridge, MA: Belknap Press, 2009.

Oakes, James. *Freedom National: The Destruction of Slavery in the United States 1861–1865*. New York: W. W. Norton, 2013.

Smock, Raymond W. *Booker T. Washington: Black Leadership in the Age of Jim Crow*. Chicago, IL: Ivan R. Dee, 2009.

Sugrue, Thomas J. *Sweet Land of Liberty: The Forgotten Struggle for Civil Rights in the North*. New York: Random House, 2008.

Tell, Bernice. "Separate but One: Booker T. Washington's 'Atlanta Compromise' Displayed at Library." *Library of Congress Information Bulletin*, February 19, 1996. https://www.loc.gov/loc/lcib/9603/booker.html.

Tuskegee University. "Dr. Booker Taliaferro Washington." https://www.tuskegee.edu/discover-tu/tu-presidents/booker-t-washington.

Washington, Booker T. "Address at the Opening of the International Cotton States Exposition, Atlanta, Georgia, September 18, 1895." Library of Congress, American Memory. https://memory.loc.gov/cgi-bin/query/r?ammem/murray:@field(DOCID+@lit(lcrbmrpt0c15div4)).

———. "The Awakening of the Negro." *Atlantic*, September 1896. https://www.theatlantic.com/magazine/archive/1896/09/the-awakening-of-the-negro/305449.

————. Story of My Life and Work: An Autobiography. Toronto, Canada: J. L. Nichols and Company, 1901. From the University of North Carolina at Chapel Hill Collection "Documenting the American South," 1999. http://www.btwsociety.org/library/books/Story_of_My_Life/16.php.

————. *Up from Slavery.* Oxford, UK: Oxford University Press, 1995.

INDEX

ABOUT THE AUTHOR

Avery Elizabeth Hurt is the author of many books for children and young adults. She lives less than 150 miles (241 kilometers) from Tuskegee, Alabama. As dedicated home gardeners, she and her husband have benefited greatly from the work of Booker T. Washington by reading and learning from many of the agricultural bulletins published by Tuskegee University.